KU-467-406

Collins *Little book of*

SCRABBLE

BRAND Crossword Game

SECRETS

Mark Nyman

HarperCollins Publishers
Westerhill Road
Bishopbriggs
Glasgow
G64 2QT

First edition 2011

Reprint 10 9 8 7 6 5 4 3 2 1 0

© HarperCollins Publishers 2011

ISBN 978-0-00-744314-7

www.collinslanguage.com

A catalogue record for this book is
available from the British Library

Typeset by Davidson Publishing
Solutions, Glasgow

Printed and bound at Leo Paper
Products Ltd

Editor
Freddy Chick

For the Publisher
Lucy Cooper
Kerry Ferguson
Elaine Higgleton

Foreword

Mark Nyman is pretty cool, off and on the Scrabble board. He takes the game seriously but also gets a lot of fun out of it.

I was in the audience when Mark won the 1993 World Championships and he remains the only UK player to have achieved this feat. As a sports enthusiast, I've been to a few sporting events – Wimbledon Finals, World Cup Cricket etc. I can honestly say that I've never experienced an atmosphere like the one when, trailing two games to one in a best of five final to the Canadian Joel Wapnick, Mark recovered from a 180 point deficit in the 4th game to win that game by just 7 points and then went on to take the title. Yes, people were standing on their seats and cheering over a game of Scrabble!

I was also at the 1999 World Final where he lost the deciding game to the same opponent by just one point.

Uniquely amongst the best players in the world, Mark has experienced the highs and lows of Scrabble at its ultimate level but he has retained his passion and joy for the game. This comes across, in spades, in this short but comprehensive book which is aimed at beginners but has something for players of all abilities, even if it's just the 'Skulduggery' section, which is a must-read!

Philip Nelkon
Scrabble Promotions Manager – Mattel

Essential Scrabble Glossary

Hooks are words than can be transformed into another valid word by the addition of a single letter at the beginning or the end. For example:

EARFUL can take a **T** at the front to make **TEARFUL**

SEA can take a **T** at the end to make **SEAT**

Blockers are words which cannot have a letter added to either the front or the beginning. As you cannot play onto either the beginning or the end of blockers, they often 'close down' part of the board.

Floaters are letters that are available on the board for you to use as part of another word, and to play onto.

1 | Two's Company

Scrabble study always starts with the 2-letter words. The most useful of these are the ones with the highest-scoring letters, i.e. the Q and Z. So let's begin with the three most useful words in Scrabble:

QI   Life force
ZA   Pizza
ZO   Himalayan cattle

So if an I, A or O is directly below or to the right of a triple letter square, you could place the Q or Z on it and, if you can go across/down with the same word, a potential 62 points can be picked up, much to the consternation of your opponent!

2 Less is More

A common myth amongst Scrabble beginners is that the longer the word, the higher the score – this is not necessarily true at all.

You may **AGONIZE** for as little as 17 if you don't make good use of the premium squares, whereas as in secret 1 a simple **ZO** or **ZA** might get you 62 on the same turn – be economical with your tiles.

3 Starters

S, C and P respectively are the most common starting letters and together comprise over a quarter of the words in the dictionary. So when moving your rack around it's a good idea to put them at the beginning – a profusion of words arise from such useful prefixes as:

SEMI-, SUB-

CH-, CO-

POLY-, PRE-

4 | Meaning-less?

Whether or not to insist on knowing the meanings of words played is a controversial topic and can lead to lots of arguments.

The official rule is that you don't have to know them, but some people still think it's just not right. If you are playing at home and insist on knowing the meanings it can lead to trouble because it's a moot point how close you have to get to the exact definition. For example, you may play **ZLOTY** knowing it's a type of currency, but your opponent may insist on you explaining from which country it originates. If you don't know, will they let you have the word?

These inconsistencies can cause a fallout, so far better to stick to the 'not having to know' rule for peace's sake. It's great to find out the meanings, but when there are 140,000 Scrabble words with 9 letters or less, it would take an incredible mind to know every meaning as well as every word.

Personally, I would rather learn a new word than a meaning of an existing word I know (shock horror), but I do enjoy picking up some of the meanings along the way. The World Champion – Pakorn Nemitrmansuk from Thailand – struggles with fluent English and doesn't bother with the meanings of the more outlandish words.

On the other hand, Scrabble is a great learning tool for improving vocabulary so at the end of the day, whatever floats your boat. Just don't sneer at your opponent if they don't know a definition unless you think they'd do the same to you.

5 | PARDON ME

The 6-letter combination **PARDON** goes with every vowel to make an unusual 7-letter word and thereby give a possible 50-point bonus:

PARDON + A   PANDORA – sea bream
+ E   PADRONE – Italian inn owner
+ I   PONIARD – dagger
+ O   PANDOOR – a force of brutal Croatian soldiers
+ U   PANDOUR – " " " "

By the way **PARDON ME** is an anagram of **POMANDER**.

6 | Central Perk

If you are playing the first move, always place your highest-scoring letter on the double letter square if you have a 5-letter word or longer to play. Also, try to avoid placing the vowels directly above and below the double letter squares around the centre square. For example, **HEARD** is better than **HARED** as the R will go above/below the double letter square, rather than the E – this gives your opponent less scope for a high scoring comeback play.

7

There are no less than thirteen different variations of the word **HELLO**:

HALLO

HALLALOO

HALLOA

HALLOO

HILLO

HILLOA

HOLLA

HOLLO

HOLLOA

HOLLOO

HULLO

HULLOA

HULLOO

They are all verbs (apart from **HALLALOO**) and **HALLOES**, **HELLOES**, **HILLOES**, **HOLLOES** and **HULLOES** are also okay, so there are forty-five derivatives altogether.

8 | Irritable Vowel Syndrome

Too many vowels on your rack can lead to disaster. Generally, the ideal ratio of consonants to vowels is 4:3. So having four vowels is a slight overload but fairly easily remedied – five or more and the alarm bells start ringing.

In this case, it can take two or three turns to restore the balance, and the worst of it is you are unlikely to score well in the meantime since the vowels are worth only one point at face value.

Here are some examples of lovely **vowelly** words to get you out of trouble quickly:

AE	one
AI	slow moving shaggy South American animal
EA	a river
IO	moth
OI	shout for attention
OU	man
AIA	Eastern female servant
AUA	mullet
AUE	Maori exclamation
EAU	a river
EUOI	a cry of Bacchic frenzy
EUOUAE	" " " " "

It's amazing how often **EUOI** especially comes up – those followers of Bacchus had some fun didn't they?

9 | Ⓐ **Fine Mess**

You can easily get out of a sticky situation with multiple
Ⓐs if you know some of these:

AA	volcanic lava
AAL	Asian tree
ABA	Syrian camel-haired cloth
AKA	New Zealand vine
ALA	wing
AMA	water vessel
ANA	collection of reminiscences
AVA	Polynesian shrub
AWA	away
CAA	to call
FAA	fall
MAA	to bleat
ACAI	Brazilian berry
ANOA	small cattle
ATUA	demon
AULA	hall
ABACA	Philippine plant
ALAAP	Indian rhythm
ALAPA	" "
ANANA	pineapple
ARABA	Asian carriage
TAATA	father
ARAARA	game fish
TAIAHA	Maori staff

⒠ is the most common letter and the best vowel to hold. You can really struggle with a dearth of ⒠s in the game – they are its lifeblood – but on the flip side, you don't really want more than a couple on your rack at any one time. Because there are twelve in the set, you can quite often find yourself with three or four ⒠s – here are a few words to ⒠s the problem:

EE	eye
EEN	eyes
EME	uncle
ENE	even
JEE	to move ahead
MEE	Malaysian noodle dish
EEVEN	evening
ELPEE	long-playing record
ETWEE	small case
EXEME	to set free
GELEE	jelly
ENTETE	obsessed
VEEPEE	vice president
VENEWE	venue

Do however try and keep one ⒠ back on your rack unless the score with it is too good to miss.

It's amazing how regularly you can get stuck with two or three I s on your rack and, if you're not careful, the problem can persist. To dig you out of the I -hole sooner rather than later, try playing the following:

IWI	Maori tribe	**WILI**	spirit
BIDI	Indian cigarette	**AALII**	bushy shrub
DIVI	stupid person	**BIKIE**	motorcycle gang member
FIFI	mountaineering hook	**CIVIE**	civilian
FINI	finish	**DIXIE**	cooking pot
HILI	scar on a seed	**FIXIT**	solution to a problem
IMID	a drug		
INIA	points at the back of the head	**LITAI**	Lithuanian monetary unit
IRID	iris	**MIRIN**	Japanese rice wine
IXIA	African plant	**OIDIA**	fungal spores
LIRI	monetary unit	**TEIID**	lizard
NIDI	insects' nests	**VISIE**	to look
PILI	Philippine tree	**YITIE**	bunting
TITI	South American monkey	**ZIMBI**	cowrie shell

O My Word

A surfeit of Os is relatively easy to alleviate, but here's a soupçon of gems to make it even simpler:

OO	wool
OBO	ship carrying oil
ONO	Hawaiian fish
OOM	old man's title of respect
OOR	our
OOT	out
OXO	acid containing oxygen
OLIO	dish of differing ingredients
ORZO	pasta
OVOLO	convex moulding
GOOROO	guru
HOOROO	hurrah

13 | U-seless

The U is by far the least useful of the vowels, unless of course accompanied by the Q. More than one U can really cramp your style and flow, but there are a few unusual multiple-U words that can help:

ULU	knife
UMU	oven
UTU	reward
BUBU	African garment
HUHU	hairy New Zealand beetle
KURU	nervous disease
LULU	outstanding person
PUPU	Hawaiian dish
RURU	owl
SULU	Fijian sarong
UNAU	two-toed sloth
URUS	extinct European ox
YUZU	citrus fruit
AHURU	Pacific cod
BUTUT	Gambian monetary unit
DURUM	Mediterranean wheat
QUIPU	Incan recording device
UHURU	national independence
URUBU	bird
MUUMUU	Hawaiian dress

14 | Vocabulary

A player's vocabulary is their ammunition in the game. It's not the 'be all and end all' but the more words you know, the more you should improve. An average person's vocabulary is between 10-15,000 words, i.e. about 10% of all the words useful to Scrabble, so there's plenty of scope for improvement.

Don't be put off at the thought of having to learn 100,000 new words. If you're willing to give it a go, you can be economical with your study as some words are a lot more 'Scrabble-friendly' than others. The best players probably know about half of them and there are only a handful of people close to knowing the lot – and they definitely need to get out more…

15 | Size Matters

The 2-letter words are the bread and butter of Scrabble, and learning them is by no means an insurmountable task. There are just 124 twos of which about a third are everyday words anyway, so learning two or three a day will crack them all in the space of a month.

Next come the 1300 or so 3-letter words. Only the top players know all these, but it's surprising how many you will pick up with practice.

The more weird and wonderful 4s and 5s are reserved for the serious player – if you're starting out on the competitive road, it's best to kick off by learning those with the high-scoring letters.

The 6's aren't as important as you might think and probably come last in a study regime. However, there are some fabulous 6-letter blockers worth knowing.

The high-probability 7s and 8s are really useful in the search for that treasured 50-point bonus. There are about 25,000 7-letter words in all and 30,000 eights, but don't let that deter you. Knowledge of the most likely 250 of each will improve your game immensely.

9-letter (or longer) words come up very rarely, though it's incredibly satisfying when they do. In terms of Scrabble study don't worry about them – that saves you looking at half the dictionary.

16 | Some Real Corkers

Here's an A to Z of some of my favourite 7s and 8s:

AZULEJO	Spanish porcelain tile
BUHUNDS	Norwegian dogs
CONEPATL	skunk
DWEEBISH	quite stupid
EUPHRASY	annual plant
FIREFANG	to overheat through decomposition
GUNKHOLE	to go on short boat excursions
HEITIKI	Maori neck ornament
ICEKHANA	motor race on frozen lake
JEREPIGO	fortified wine
KERCHOO	atishoo
LUNKHEAD	stupid person
MRIDANGA	Indian drum
NUDZHES	nudges
OLYCOOK	American doughnut
PATOOTIE	person's bottom
QUETZAL	Central American bird
RUDESBY	rude person
SLYBOOTS	sly person
TAGHAIRM	divination sought by lying in a bullock's hide under a Scottish waterfall

UNSHRUBD	not having shrubs
VEEJAYS	video jockeys
WOSBIRD	illegitimate child
XERAFIN	Indian coin
YAHOOISM	crudeness
ZEDOARY	Asian stem used as a stimulant

17 | Time for a C H A₁ N G₂ E₁

There is a great deal of skill in choosing the right time to change your letters, as well as which ones to throw back in the bag.

The first, and most important, tip on this subject is **DON'T BE AFRAID TO CHANGE.** You may score zero on that particular turn, but if the alternative is to be left with a horrible combination of letters, like I I I U V V W, you may get stuck scoring ten points per move for several turns. Say you average twenty points per turn, it's better to change and score a likely sixty over the next three moves than forty without the change.

Hold on to your
R E T S I N A

The most 50-point bonus-conducive letters are **AEINRST** – generally, when throwing tiles in the bag, you want to keep one of any of these that you hold on your rack, as long as you leave a decent consonant to vowel ratio (i.e. 3:2, 2:2, 2:1, 1:1). The highest scoring letters **JQXZ** are only worth keeping if there are some tasty triple-letter and triple-word squares available to play onto the board. If the board is tight and especially if there are no floating vowels, the high-scorers could be rendered useless. The X and Z are generally more fruitful than the J and Q if you can't resist holding one back.

19 | Chuck 'em In

In my opinion, the converse of **AEINRST** is **FGJQUVW** – i.e. these are the seven worst letters in the set. So, when changing, always get rid of these unless you have the Q with a **U**, a high-scoring place for the J, or a promising -ING combination. Even then you might be held back, especially if the board is tight.

You may be surprised about the inclusion of the G, but in my experience Gs are generally bad news. If you're deciding to change, always throw back a V if you have one – that's the weakest letter of all, partly because it's the only one that doesn't form a 2-letter word. As for the rest – **-BCDHKLMOPXYZ** – they all have their merits and it depends on the state of the board as to whether any of them are worth keeping – usually chuck though.

20 To the MAX

MAX- is a handy prefix and produces some lovely extensions:

MAXED	reached full extent
MAXI	large racing yacht
MAXICOAT	long coat
MAXILLA	upper jawbone
MAXIMIN	highest of set of minimum values
MAXIMITE	explosive
MAXIMUS	method rung on twelve bells
MAXING	reaching full extent
MAXIXE	Brazilian dance
MAXWELL	unit of magnetic flux

There's also **SUPERMAX** – relating to the very highest levels of security.

21 | Leave No STONE Unturned

Here's a selection of words to a-stone-ish you:

ASTONE	astonish
BURSTONE	hard rock
CAMSTONE	limestone
EARSTONE	calcium carbonate crystal in the ear
HISTONE	DNA protein
ICESTONE	cryolite
LAPSTONE	cobbler's device
POTSTONE	used for making cooking vessels
ROESTONE	limestone
RUBSTONE	used for sharpening
STONERAG	lichen
STONERAW	lichen
SUNSTONE	feldspar
TINSTONE	black or brown stone

There's also the 9-letter **IRONSTONE**, which is a very nice anagram of **SEROTONIN**, and **LIMESTONE** and **MILESTONE** are both anagrams of **LEMONIEST**.

22 Take the Rough with the Smooth

Certain mini-combinations of consonants work really well together and are worth holding on to in the search for a 50-point bonus. They often tend to comprise both 'hard' and 'soft' letters but it's best not to keep back all 'hard' letters together and likewise all 'soft'.

'Hard' consonants **BDFGJKPQTVX**
'Soft' consonants **HLMNRSWYZ**

I've left out **C** as it can be both 'soft' and 'hard' – this adaptability is why it's a particular favourite.

So..........

In-Consonants

Consonant combinations particularly worth keeping back for potential bonus play:

BL, BM, BR, CH, CK, CN, CL, CR, CT, DL, DN, DR, HP, KL, KN, KR, LP, MP, NT, PR, RT

BDR, BLR, BMR, CDR, CHN, CHR, CHT, CLR, CLT, CNR, CNT, CRT, DLR, DNR, DPR, DRT, GLN, GNR, HPR, HNP, HPT, KLN, KLR, KNR, KNT, LPR, LPT, NRT, PRT

An **S** is always worth holding on to in addition to these combinations. You will see they all contain at least one 'hard' and one 'soft' letter.

Not In-Consonants

Consonant combinations to avoid (using 3-point or lower tiles):

BG, **BP**, **CG**, **DT**, **GP**, **GT**, **LN**.

BDT, **BGP**, **BGT**, **BPT**, **DGT**, **DGP**, **GPT**, **LNR**.

You will notice that all these contain either all 'soft' or all 'hard' letters. Of course, any combination with two of the same letter and you automatically look to offload the duplicate.

25 | **Licence to Thrill**

It can be good anagram practice to look at car number plates and try to find the shortest word you can using all the letters within them. Add any extra letters you want but the less the better, for example:

SKO5 CYJ   **JOCKEYS** (beats **JOYSTICK**)
NCL2 END   **INCLINED** (beats **DECLINING**)
OWO6 ETA   **TEAKWOOD** (beats **TAEKWONDO**)

This can be great fun and very satisfying on a long car journey but don't forget to concentrate on the road as well. Of course, you won't be able to find a word with all the plates – if you see QXO7 GJZ, give up immediately and move on to the next car.

There are some gorgeous 7- and 8-letter anagram pairs – here are some of my favourites:

APPRIZE	**ZAPPIER**
BOGEYMAN	**MONEYBAG**
CRUMPETS	**SPECTRUM**
DOORBELL	**BORDELLO**
ELATION	**TOENAIL**
FLUSHING	**LUNGFISH** (freshwater fish)
GHETTOED	**DOGTEETH** (carved ornaments)
HOGMANAY	**MAHOGANY**
IFFIEST	**FIFTIES**
JITTERS	**TRIJETS** (jets with three engines)
KIDNAPS	**SKIDPAN** (slippery area)
LIMEADE	**EMAILED**
MOORHEN	**HORMONE**
NAPPIES	**PINESAP** (red herb)
OOMPAHS	**SHAMPOO**
PRESUME	**SUPREME**
QUERIES	**ESQUIRE**
RINGTONE	**NITROGEN**
SCREWTOP	**CROWSTEP** (set of steps to the top of a gable)

TAPEWORM	**POMWATER** (kind of apple)
UTOPIAN	**OPUNTIA** (cactus)
VIOLATED	**DOVETAIL**
WASPNEST	**STEWPANS**
XEROTIC	**EXCITOR** (nerve)
YACKERS	**SCREAKY**
ZINCITE	**CITIZEN**

XEROTIC is not as kinky as it sounds – it relates to dryness of bodily tissues.

Americanisms

As a general rule, all US alternative spellings are allowed in Scrabble, so color, humor, neighbor etc are OK – like it or not. Also, almost every **–ISE** verb can be spelt with **–IZE**. It's interesting that Collins Dictionary is recognised everywhere in the World as the English Scrabble 'bible', apart from the US and Canada, where they use Webster's. Since Collins incorporates all of Webster's and a lot more, you ironically need to unlearn loads of words to play in the States. This seems a reflection of the US 'we are the world' attitude, so don't bother playing serious Scrabble over there.

South America is a relatively unexplored continent dictionary wise – there's plenty of scope for future great words from that neck of the woods.

28 | Monkey Business

Monkeys keep ape-earing in the dictionary:

BANDARI	MICO
CEBID	OUAKARI
COAITA	OUISTITI
DOUC	SAGOUIN
ENTELLUS	SAIMIRI
GRIVET	SAJOU
GUEREZA	TALAPOIN
HANUMAN	TAMARIN
JOCKO	VERVET
LANGUR	WANDEROO
MANGABEY	ZATI

The beautiful **CYNOMOLGI** has to be worth a mention, however unlikely it is to jump out at you.

29 Slanguage

Slang words are perfectly allowable in Scrabble when they become common English usage. A lot of Australian slang appears, such as:

ALF	an uncultivated Australian
SIK	excellent
ACCA	an academic
ALKO	alcoholic
DACK	to forcefully remove trousers
DOCO	documentary
DORB	stupid person
DRAC	unattractive woman
GOOG	egg
KERO	kerosene
KYBO	temporary camping lavatory
MYXO	myxomatosis
NOAH	shark
UMPY	umpire
WARB	insignificant person
FIRIE	firefighter
NIXER	spare-time job
UMPIE	umpire

SLANGUAGE is a word in itself – a lovely front hook to 'language'.

Feathered Friends

There are plenty of exotic **-BIRD** words to fly by you:

AXEBIRD	nightjar
BOOBIRD	person who boos
COWBIRD	American songbird
FATBIRD	nocturnal bird
GAOLBIRD	person confined to jail
HANGBIRD	bird that builds a hanging nest
JAYBIRD	jay
KINGBIRD	American flycatcher
LYREBIRD	Australian bird that spreads its tail into shape of a lyre
MAYBIRD	American songbird
OVENBIRD	small South American bird
PUFFBIRD	tropical American bird
RICEBIRD	bird frequenting rice fields
SNOWBIRD	cocaine addict
WHIPBIRD	whistling bird
YARDBIRD	inexperienced soldier

31 | Abbreviations and Acronyms

Abbreviations are not allowed in themselves unless they come into common conversation, in which case they become colloquialisms, for example **AD** for advertisement. The same applies to acronyms – there are a few crackers:

ASPRO	associate professor
BAMBI	born-again middle-aged biker
ELINT	electronic intelligence
FEDEX	federal express
JATO	jet-assisted take-off
MIPS	million instructions per second
NOX	nitrogen oxide
POMO	post-modernism
QUANGO	quasi-autonomous non-governmental organisation
RONZER	someone from rest of New Zealand – not Auckland
TASER	Thomas A. Swift's electric rifle
TWOCCER	taking without owner's consent
WAAC	member of Women's Auxiliary Arms Corps
WOOPIE	well-off older person
YABA	yet another bloody acronym!

32 | The Blank

The blank is without doubt the best tile in the Scrabble set. If you're lucky enough to get both during the course of the game it will increase your chances of winning hugely, but you need to make the most of them.

If you get a blank early on, try and save it until you can use it in a 50-point bonus word. Never waste it on a move scoring less than 30 points.

Some players get really stuck when a blank appears – it's not surprising when you consider there are effectively twenty-six combinations to think about. But try to envisage the blank as a particular letter on your rack – some are more likely to go well with your other six letters than others. Even so, moves with a blank tend to require a great deal more thought and it's understandable they take longer.

As a general rule, use the blank when your move scores over 20 points more than one without it. Otherwise, hold on for a big play later – it's worth the wait.

Two blanks together can be a real mind-blower as there are 676 potential combinations. Don't panic: the more you play, the more you'll get a feel for which letters you're looking for them to be.

33 | **Bonus Play**

If you can play out all your letters for the 50-point bonus, you'll enhance your winning chances enormously. Achieving this once in a game is good, twice excellent and three or more times will almost guarantee you victory.

The art of bonus finding is innate to Scrabble success – much of it is to do with rack-balancing along with knowing some high-probability 7- and 8-letter words (i.e. those with the most common letters) to help find that killer move.

There are some great 6- and 7-letter combinations to work towards to give yourself the best opportunity of making it happen.

34 Another R E T S I N A

As well as having nine anagrams (you don't need to know them all), **RETSINA** goes with more letters to make an 8-letter word than any other – so look for these floaters on the board:

A. **ARTESIAN** (well)

B. **BANISTER**

C. **CANISTER**

D. **STRAINED**

E. **TRAINEES**

F. **FENITARS**
(European plants)

G. **ANGRIEST**

H. **HAIRNETS**

I. **RAINIEST**

J. **NARTJIES**
(tangerines)

K. **NARKIEST**

L. **ENTRAILS**

M. **MINARETS**

N. **TRANNIES**

O. **NOTARIES**

P. **PAINTERS**

R. **TRAINERS**

S. **STAINERS**

T. **NITRATES**

U. **URINATES**

W. **TINWARES**
(objects made of
tin plate)

ANTIES in your Panties

The 6-letter combination **ANTIES** goes with more letters to make a 7-letter word than any other:

A. **ENTASIA** (convex curve)

B. **BASINET** (medieval helmet)

C. **CINEAST** (film enthusiast)

D. **DETAINS**

E. **ETESIAN** (Mediterranean wind)

F. **FAINEST** (most eager)

G. **SEATING**

H. **SHEITAN** (Muslim demon)

I. **ISATINE** (yellowish-red compound)

J. **JANTIES** (petty officers)

K. **INTAKES**

L. **ENTAILS**

M. **INMATES**

N. **INANEST**

O. **ATONIES** (lack of muscle tone)

P. **PANTIES**

R. **RETSINA**

S. **NASTIES**

T. **INSTATE**

U. **AUNTIES**

V. **NATIVES**

W. **TAWNIES**

X. **SEXTAIN** (Italian verse)

Z. **ZANIEST**

So only **Q** and **Y** don't work. Note that there are several anagrams in some cases but knowing one is often enough.

36 | SEATING Room Only

SEATING is the most prolific 7-letter word when it comes to anagrams – it has ten:

EASTING	distance eastwards
EATINGS	
GAINEST	straightest
GENISTA	member of broom family
INGATES	entrances
INGESTA	nourishment
TAGINES	African cooking pots
TANGIES	Orkney water spirits
TEASING	
TSIGANE	Gypsy music

37 | M A N -alive

-MAN is a very productive suffix – here are some 7s and 8s you might not expect:

ADWOMAN	woman working in advertising
BRIDEMAN	bridegroom's attendant
CHOREMAN	handyman
DRAGOMAN	Middle Eastern guide
EARTHMAN	inhabitant of the earth
FACEMAN	miner working at coalface
GLEEMAN	minstrel
HELIMAN	helicopter pilot
IRONMAN	very strong man
JURYMAN	member of a jury
KEELMAN	bargeman
LOCOMAN	railwayman
MOTORMAN	driver of electric train
OVERSMAN	overseer
PRIZEMAN	winner of prize
QUILLMAN	clerk
RADIOMAN	radio operator
SWEETMAN	Caribbean man kept by a woman
TOYWOMAN	woman who sells toys
UNWOMAN	to remove womanly qualities from
VERSEMAN	man who writes verse
WATERMAN	skilled boatman
YEGGMAN	burglar

38 | De-stress

Part of the attraction of Scrabble is it helps you forget about your worries while you're concentrating on the game. Here are a few suggestions to make it an even more relaxing and positive experience:

(a) Sleep well the night before – a couple of beers or glasses of wine should do the trick

(b) Drink caffeine to stimulate your brain – not too much though as it might get a bit wayward

(c) Drink water – again in moderation as needing the loo will make you lose concentration

(d) Have a massage

(e) Play uplifting music

(f) Avoid stressful work and particularly bad bosses

(g) Avoid affairs

(h) Play in pleasant uncluttered surroundings

(i) Laugh at your opponent if they are over-competitive

(j) Support a winning football team, i.e. Barcelona or QPR

W O O D you believe it?

WOOD works really well as a prefix and suffix:

AGALWOOD	Asian tree
BEARWOOD	bark used as a laxative
CAMWOOD	W. African tree
DAGWOOD	European shrub
ELMWOOD	wood from elm tree
FATWOOD	kindling
GUMWOOD	gumtree
HAREWOOD	sycamore
INKWOOD	tree
KINGWOOD	wood of Brazilian leguminous tree
LATEWOOD	formed later in tree's growing season
MILKWOOD	tree producing latex
NUTWOOD	walnut
OVENWOOD	word for burning in oven
PEARWOOD	wood from pear tree
SAPWOOD	soft wood beneath bark
WILDWOOD	forest growing in natural uncultivated state
WOODBIN	box for firewood
WOODFREE	paper from treated pulp
WOODHEN	flightless bird
WOODLORE	woodcraft skills
WOODMEAL	sawdust powder
WOODMICE	field mice

WOODNESS	quality of wood
WOODNOTE	natural musical note
WOODROOF	plant
WOODSIA	fern
WOODSIER	more connected with woods
WOODSKIN	canoe made of bark
WOODTONE	colour matching that of wood
WOODWALE	green woodpecker
WOODWARD	person in charge of wood
WOODWOSE	hairy wild man of the woods

Against All Odds

ANTI- as a prefix gives rise to plenty of high-probability 7s and 8s – the meanings are mainly self-explanatory:

ANTIACNE

ANTIBOSS

ANTICOLD

ANTIDORA (bread used in Russian Orthodox Communion)

ANTIFOG

ANTIGANG

ANTIJAM

ANTIKING (a rival to an established king)

ANTILEAK

ANTIMALE

ANTINUKE

ANTIPOT

ANTIROCK (preventing a vehicle from rocking)

ANTISNOB

ANTITAX

ANTIWEED

41 | **Cheats Never Prosper**

Cheating is a very tricky subject to cover. If you're just playing a casual game at home with a like-minded individual, cheating can be fun. However, if there is any degree of competitiveness involved – DON'T CHEAT – it will only end in tears.

The obvious way to cheat is to take a very subtle peep in the bag while (hopefully) your adversary is not looking – you can avoid this by insisting the bag stays above your shoulder when picking tiles. There are all sorts of house rules to combat any shenanigans, but in tournament play there have been several instances of players being banned when caught cheating.

In one event, the deathly hush of the playing area was interrupted by the organiser announcing in front of 200 people that someone had been found out – he was literally frogmarched out of the room by a security guard, never to be seen again…

Obviously, friendly games are a different matter, but if there's any potential of upsetting your opponent rather than humouring them, don't bother.

In any case bad karma will get you in the end.

42 | **Poker Face**

It can be easy to tell whether your opponent has a good or bad rack by the look on their face once they've picked their tiles, and they can give away where they want to play their next move by staring at a particular part of the board.

This doesn't matter too much in a friendly game but, if you want to win, it will help your cause to watch out for the giveaway signs, and not react to your own letters either facially or verbally.

You could actually try doing the opposite and, for example, moan when you get good letters, but that's when you get into gamesmanship and it's a little bit unnecessary, unless you think your opponent would do the same to you.

43 Know Your

Try studying these to some degree:

AEROLOGY	study of	the atmosphere
AGROLOGY	" "	soils
AREOLOGY		Mars
APIOLOGY		bees
BATOLOGY		brambles
CETOLOGY		whales
CHAOLOGY		chaos theory
DEMOLOGY	demography	
DOXOLOGY	short hymn	
ENOLOGY	study of wine	
ETIOLOGY	" "	causes of diseases
FETOLOGY		the foetus
MENOLOGY	religious calendar	
MISOLOGY	hatred of reasoned argument	
MIXOLOGY	the art of mixing cocktails	
NOOLOGY	study of intuition	
NOMOLOGY	" "	law
NOSOLOGY		classification of diseases
OENOLOGY		more wine
OINOLOGY		even more wine
OOLOGY		birds' eggs

OREOLOGY	mountains
PEDOLOGY	children
PELOLOGY	mud therapy
PENOLOGY	punishment
RHEOLOGY	matter in physics
SEXOLOGY	human sexual behaviour
SINOLOGY	Chinese culture
SITOLOGY	food
UFOLOGY	UFOs
VINOLOGY	vines
VIROLOGY	viruses

OLOGY itself is also perfectly acceptable – it has a rather less cerebral anagram.

44 | Suffixes

Here are twenty combinations to look out for and put at the end of your rack since they are very fruitful suffixes:

-ABLE	**-ITE**
-AGE	**-IVE**
-ATE	**-IZE**
-ED	**-LESS**
-ER	**-LY**
-IC	**-MAN**
-IEST	**-MEN**
-ING	**-NESS**
-ISM	**-OUS**
-ISE	**-TION**

45 | E S S -ential

Apart from the blank, **S** is the best letter in the Scrabble set, since it starts and ends more words than any other. It should be savoured and ideally kept back to use in a bonus-word – certainly try not to use it unless you can score over 30-points. A good guide is to play it only if the score using it is at least 10-points more than the best score without.

Bear in mind though that multiple **S**s on your rack can hold you up. They're not as good together as you may think and if you have two it's normally best to offload one as soon as you can – you should still be able to achieve this with a decent score, but do hold the remaining one back for something special later.

There's a multitude of surprisingly allowable **non**-words:

NONACTOR	person who is not an actor
NONBANK	business providing similar services to a bank
NONCOLA	soft drink other than cola
NONDRUG	not involving use of drugs
NONELITE	not elite
NONFUEL	not relating to fuel
NONGUILT	innocence
NONHARDY	fragile
NONIMAGE	person who is not a celebrity
NONJURY	trial without a jury
NONLEAFY	not leafy
NONMETRO	not metropolitan
NONNEWS	not concerned with the news
NONOILY	not oily
NONPARTY	not connected with a political party
NONQUOTA	not included in a quota
NONRIGID	not rigid
NONSELF	foreign molecule in the body
NONTIDAL	not having a tide
NONURBAN	rural
NONVITAL	not vital
NONWAGE	not part of wages
NONZERO	not equal to zero

NONWORDS is in the dictionary as well.

47 | **Play to the Board**

A common error among players is to spend all their time looking at their rack rather than the board. It's all very well spotting great words with the tiles in front of you but not much use if there's nowhere to place them. You're far better off spending 90% of your time focusing on the board and its possibilities, trying if you can to keep your letters in your head simultaneously.

Adapting to this '**visual switch**' is very important and can save you a lot of brain energy as well as improve your game. It's not a simple change to achieve, so keep consciously trying to 'catch yourself on' when overfocusing on your rack.

48 | **Blocking and Opening**

Block when ahead, open when behind. That's the general rule. However, you need to be careful you don't sacrifice too many points just to block, or you may find your lead diminishes sooner than you think. Likewise, you need to open up carefully and too small a score may leave your deficit too great.

Ideally, if you can block and score over 20 points simultaneously when ahead it's worth doing; if you're behind and can open the board for at least 15 points then again go for it.

49 Set-ups

Unlike chess where you have to think about twenty moves ahead, Scrabble is all about maximising your score over your current move as well as the potential score on the next move. This can be achieved with good **rack balancing** to edge you towards that elusive 50-point bonus word, and **set-up** plays.

If you have a high-scoring J, Q, X or Z for example, and nowhere really worthwhile to play it, you may be able to set up a big score next turn by placing one of your vowels next to a premium square. Alternatively, you could set up a **hook** by holding back a letter that goes on the beginning or end of the word you play.

For example, if you have **GHORTUZ**, it might be worth playing **ROUGH** keeping back the T for the front hook next time (it goes on the end as well) – even better if adjacent to the O of **ROUGH** is a premium square to set up **ZO** for an alternative big score next time.

Try not to make the set-up too obvious though and play straight into the hands of your opponent, but it's all about giving yourself future opportunities and when they come off it's extremely satisfying.

50 By Hook or by Crook

Knowing your **hooks** can give you a great advantage over your adversary. Here's an A to Z of great front hooks of 2-letter words:

A-ZO	containing the divalent group N:N	**L**-AH	sixth degree of music scale
B-OH	exclamation to startle someone	**M**-HO	SI unit of conductance
C-HE	pronoun meaning "I"	**N**-OX	nitrogen oxide
D-IT	to stop something happening	**O**-BE	Laconian village
E-ME	uncle	**P**-AX	kiss of peace
F-OY	loyalty	**Q**-IS	energies
G-IF	if	**R**-EM	dose of radiation
H-EH	exclamation of surprise	**S**-HA	be quiet
I-TA	type of palm	**T**-EF	African grass
J-OR	movement in Indian music	**U**-DO	Japanese plant
K-HI	Greek letter	**V**-IN	French wine
		W-OF	fool
		X-IS	Greek letters
		Y-GO	past participle of go
		Z-EL	Turkish cymbal

S U P E R Words

There are also some wonderful words using the prefix
SUPER-. Here are a few examples of 8-letter words that
may help get you that elusive 50-point bonus (you can guess
the definitions!):

SUPERBAD

SUPERCAR

SUPERCOW

SUPERFAN

SUPERGUN

SUPERHOT

SUPERJET

SUPERLOO

SUPERMOM

SUPERSPY

52 | **More Vowel Trouble**

This list of 3-vowelled 4-letter words will solve your
vowel-heavy rack problems quickly and save you scoring
measly amounts for several turns in a row:

AIGA	family	**KAIE**	key
AINE	male elder	**MEOU**	to meow
AITU	half-human half-divine being	**MOAI**	Easter Island stone figures
AJEE	awry	**MOOI**	pleasing
ALAE	wings	**NAOI**	ancient temples
AMIA	fish	**OBIA**	a spell
AUNE	measure of length	**ODEA**	buildings for musical performances
AWEE	for a short time		
EALE	Roman beast	**OGEE**	moulding
EAVE	to form eaves	**OHIA**	Hawaiian plant
EINE	eyes	**ONIE**	any
EMEU	emu	**OUMA**	grandmother
EOAN	relating to the dawn	**OUPA**	grandfather
ETUI	small ornamented case	**PAUA**	New Zealand shellfish
EUGE	well done	**QUAI**	quay
EVOE	cry of Bacchic frenzy	**TOEA**	monetary unit of Papua New Guinea
HUIA	extinct New Zealand bird		
		UNAI	two-toed sloth
IDEE	idea	**URAO**	mineral
ILIA	plural of ilium	**UVEA**	part of the eyeball
IURE	by law	**VIAE**	roads
		ZOEA	crab larva

53 S U B -mission

SUB- gives rise to some under-ful words:

SUBAREA	area within a larger area
SUBBREED	breed within a larger breed
SUBCOOL	to make colder
SUBDWARF	star smaller than a dwarf star
SUBERECT	not quite erect
SUBFLOOR	rough floor
SUBGOAL	secondary goal
SUBHEAD	heading of a subsection
SUBIDEA	secondary idea
SUBLEVEL	subdivision of a level
SUBMENU	further options within computer menu
SUBNICHE	subdivision of a niche
SUBOCEAN	beneath the ocean
SUBPANEL	panel that is part of a larger panel
SUBRACE	a race considered to be inferior
SUBSONG	subdued birdsong
SUBTUNIC	garment worn under a tunic
SUBUNIT	distinct part of something larger
SUBVICAR	vicar's assistant
SUBWORLD	underworld
SUBZONE	subdivision of a zone

54 It's only a Game

At whatever level you're playing, it's easy to be a good winner but not so a good loser. Don't get too far away from the fact that Scrabble is fun.

There is nothing wrong with being competitive and wanting to win but, unless you really dislike your opponent, in which case you probably shouldn't be playing them in the first place, there's no reason to be a bad loser.

This is often a maturity issue and young players will grow out of it, hopefully sooner rather than later. Sometimes it helps to learn from a particularly painful defeat. When I played in the World Championship Final in 1999, I was beaten by just one point – it hurt badly and I didn't sleep properly for a year afterwards. Whenever I lose these days, I look back and think it can't be as bad as that, and that makes me lose better.

It really isn't worth getting too worked up over – keep things in perspective and enjoy the game whatever the outcome.

55 | **Skulduggery**

If you think your opponent is capable of some underhand tactics, try some of these to give them a taste of their own medicine:

(a) Make sure they are positioned in front of a mirror so you can see what's on their rack

(b) Party hard the night before and burp alcohol fumes over them

(c) Flick bogeys in the bag to put them off when picking their tiles

(d) Click your knuckles

(e) Cough a lot

(f) Eat lots of garlic

(g) Don't wash for a month before game

(h) Hum

(i) Grind teeth

(j) Eat baked beans and cauliflower before game and shoot off some silent-but-violents

I must thank my siblings for these suggestions – I would never have thought of them myself.

L.I.K.E-ability

It really is surprising how much the dictionary likes –**LIKE** as a suffix and it leads to loads of unlikely and useful words, for instance:

AUNTLIKE	**MAPLIKE**
BAGLIKE	**NIBLIKE**
CAGELIKE	**OWLLIKE**
DUNELIKE	**PEALIKE**
EARLIKE	**QUAYLIKE**
FATLIKE	**RODLIKE**
GATELIKE	**SAWLIKE**
HEADLIKE	**TEALIKE**
IVYLIKE	**URNLIKE**
JAWLIKE	**VASELIKE**
LAVALIKE	**WIGLIKE**

and I like **YLIKE** (a Spenserian form of alike).

57 | **Je Ne Regret Rien**

Nothing can be more annoying than playing your turn and then spotting a better move that you could have played immediately after when it's too late – but there's a great skill in not compounding the mistake by dwelling on it.

Your mind should be fully focused on your current move and not hampered by wondering what might have been. I remember a Mastermind contestant who was doing brilliantly at the General Knowledge round – he whizzed off ten answers in a row, then made one error which threw him completely and he got the next ten wrong.

It's much the same in Scrabble – far better to put mistakes out of your mind and move on.

Have you got what it takes?

There are plenty of attributes that go into making a good Scrabble player. Numeracy, literacy, a sound mind, enthusiasm and positivity are just some of them. Experience counts a great deal too: like everything, practice makes perfect and the more you play, the more you'll improve.

A 'killer instinct' is important if you want to take it more seriously – I hope I'm not being too controversial by saying that this tends to be inbred in men more than women, but the reason the stats show that men seem to do better is that they generally have more time on their hands.

Top players are often creative mathematicians – this may seem contradictory as most people are either one or the other, but if you're lucky enough to be talented at both, you definitely have the basic ingredients to be a Scrabble success.

Juicy J-words

Here are twenty-five tasty treats using the J:

JA	yes	**JEAT**	jet
JO	sweetheart	**JEFE**	military leader
GJU	Shetland violin	**JEON**	Korean pancake
TAJ	Muslim cap	**JIAO**	Chinese currency
BAJU	Malay jacket	**JIVY**	lively
BENJ	Indian hemp	**JOCO**	relaxed
DOJO	judo hall	**JOTA**	Spanish dance
GAJO	non-gypsy	**JUBE**	church gallery
JAAP	simpleton (*South African offensive*)	**JYNX**	woodpecker
		FALAJ	water channel
JAGA	to guard	**KANJI**	Japanese writing system
JAKE	all right		
JAXY	buttocks	**LAPJE**	rag
		PUNJI	bamboo stick

Ideally you'll be looking to use the J in conjunction with one of the premium squares, and scoring around thirty points in the process if the board is relatively open.

60 JINN and Tonic

JINN is a spirit (not the drink) in Muslim mythology, but it can be spelt in several different ways:

DJIN

DJINN

DJINNI

DJINNY

GINN

JINNEE

JINNI

Of these, only **DJIN**, **DJINN** and **JINNI** take an **S** for some reason.

To confuse you further, also allowable are **JIN** – a Chinese unit of weight – and **JINNE**, which is a South African exclamation of surprise.

The **Q** can really cramp your style during the game and it's really not worth holding on to in the hope that you pick up a **U** further down the line. However, as well as the invaluable **QI**, there are some more wonderful **U**-less **Q** words, which can come to your rescue:

FAQIR	Muslim who spurns worldly possessions	**QINTAR**	Albanian monetary unit
		QOPH	Hebrew letter
INQILAB	revolution	**QORMA**	mild Indian dish
NIQAB	Muslim veil		
QABALA	Jewish mystical tradition	**QWERTY**	keyboard
		SHEQALIM	Israeli monetary unit
QADI	Muslim judge		
QAID	chief	**SHEQEL**	Israeli monetary unit (*plural*)
QANAT	underground channel		
QASIDA	Arabic verse form	**TALAQ**	Muslim divorce
QAT	African shrub	**TRANQ**	tranquilizer
QAWWAL	Islamic singer	**TSADDIQ**	Jewish leader
QIBLA	direction of Mecca	**TZADDIQ**	" "
		WAQF	Muslim endowment
QIGONG	system of breathing and exercise	**YAQONA**	Polynesian shrub
QINDAR	Albanian monetary unit		

The X is the best of the high-scorers, largely because it goes with all the vowels to make 2-letter words:

AX axe
EX to delete
XI Greek letter
OX
XU Vietnamese currency

Always look to play it on the doubles and triples – doubling up both ways can bring you an easy thirty-two or tripling gets you forty-eight points just for the X alone.

Here are some 3-letter X-amples to help you X-cel:

DEX dextroamphetamine
DUX top school pupil
GOX gaseous oxygen
HOX hamstring
KEX plant
LEX system of laws
LOX to load with liquid oxygen
MUX to spoil
OXY ox
PIX receptacle

PYX receptacle
REX king
TEX weight unit measuring yarn density
TIX tickets
TUX tuxedo
VOX voice
WEX to wax
WOX wax
YEX to hiccup

63 **ZO Far ZO Good**

The infamous **ZO** – officially a Tibetan breed of cattle formed by crossing a yak with a cow – has ten other members of its herd:

DSO
DSOBO
DSOMO
DZO
DZHO
JOMO
ZHO
ZHOMO
ZOBO
ZOBU

Note well that the **DSOMO** and **ZHOMO** are female, while the **ZEBU** – an Asian ox with a humped back – can be seen grazing in the next field.

64 | **Enjoy the Moment**

When you spot a fantastic word or a game-winning move, just take a minute or so to savour the satisfaction, rather than play it immediately.

The uplifting feeling will seep through you – you don't have to jump up in the air or do handstands – just sit back and relax in your good vibe, whilst your opponent has absolutely no idea what's coming.

65 South African Words

Lots of South African entries have reached the dictionary in the last few years, for example:

BRU	a friend
JOL	to have a good time
SIF	nasty
BOEP	protruding belly
BOET	brother
BRAK	crossbred dog
EISH	expressing dismay
ISIT	seeking confirmation
KAAL	naked
KIFF	excellent
MOER	to attack someone
WENA	you
YEBO	yes
BRAAI	to grill over open coals
NOOIT	expressing surprise
SPAZA	township shop (*slang*)
VOEMA	vigour

66 | **More Hooks**

There are loads of handy front hooks of 3-letter words to make some really weird 4-letter words – here's just a sample:

S-**AXE**	greyish-blue colour	
K-**BAR**	kilobar	
E-**COD**	expression of surprise	
U-**DON**	Japanese noodles	
T-**EGG**	two-year-old sheep	
V-**EGO**	vegetarian	
M-**EVE**	to move	
A-**GIN**	against	
P-**HAT**	terrific	
Z-**ILL**	finger cymbal	
J-**IMP**	handsome	
T-**IVY**	at full speed	
S-**JOE**	exclamation of surprise	
K-**LAP**	to slap	

G-**LEG**	quick
S-**MEW**	a duck
E-**NOW**	enough
Y-**OWE**	ewe
A-**POD**	animal without feet
E-**REV**	day before
V-**ROT**	rotten
V-**ROW**	woman
E-**SKY**	food and drink container
E-**THE**	easy
O-**URN**	our
E-**VET**	newt
H-**WAN**	won
H-**YEN**	hyena
P-**YET**	magpie
M-**ZEE**	old person

A Young Man's Game?

Nine of the ten World Scrabble Champions have been men under 40-years old. Joel Wapnick from Canada gives hope to us all – he won the title at the age of 53 – but there's no denying agile young minds have an advantage. The best young players are from Thailand as Scrabble is included in their school curriculum as a way of teaching English. It would be lovely to see a greater Scrabble presence in UK schools as it's such a fun way to improve children's literacy and numeracy.

There are a few youth workshops and competitions over here. Having personally taught in several lunchtime and after-school clubs, I can say that the enthusiasm is tremendous. A word of advice however to the youngsters from a wise old man – "don't be too cocky and slow down a bit".

68 | More Corkers

Another alphabet of absolute beauties:

ADZUKI	leguminous plant
BLIPVERT	very short television advertisement
CHILIDOG	hot dog with chilli sauce
DRONKLAP	drunkard
EXEQUY	funeral rite
FJELD	high rocky Scandinavian plateau
GILLYVOR	carnation
HRYVNIA	money unit of Ukraine
IZVESTIA	news
JEDI	person claiming to live according to Star Wars Jedi philosophy
KUVASZ	Hungarian dog
LOGJUICE	poor quality port
MPRET	former Albanian ruler
NONG	stupid person (*Australian slang*)
OULAKAN	fish
PYENGADU	leguminous tree
QUANDONG	small Australian tree
RUBABOO	soup
STINKPOT	person that stinks

TAKIN	massive S. Asian mammal with shaggy coat and backwards and upwards horns
UINTAITE	asphalt
VOZHD	Russian leader
WAYLEGGO	away here! let go!
XENOPUS	African frog
YUTZ	fool
ZELATRIX	nun monitoring younger nuns' behaviour

Hard of Herring

-FISH is another swimmingly seaworthy suffix when you trawl through the dictionary:

BATFISH

CAVEFISH

DEALFISH

FOOLFISH

GOATFISH

HEADFISH

JEWFISH

LADYFISH

MILKFISH

NUMBFISH

OARFISH

PANFISH

ROSEFISH

STUDFISH

TUBFISH

WEAKFISH

The de-fin-itions are not in plaice: they're all types of fish.

Tile Tracking

Tracking tiles is allowable and really important if you want to get more serious. It helps to give you a rough idea of consonant to vowel ratio as the game goes on – if you find more consonants than normal have already been played for example, you may want to play less on your turn as there are comparatively less left in the bag to pick – this is really useful when it comes to balancing your rack.

However, the main point of tracking is in the endgame, especially if the scores are close. If you track correctly – which is surprisingly simple with a bit of practice – you will know what's on your opponent's rack once the bag is emptied. This allows you to spot what you think is their best move and stop them in their tracks by blocking appropriately, which could make all the difference between winning and losing.

All you need to do to tile track is write out the alphabet at the start of the game and cross off the letters as they are played. For example, if **MARK** is played on the first move, write down 8 next to your Ⓐ as there will be eight Ⓐ's left unplayed. Similarly 1 next to the Ⓜ, 5 next to the Ⓡ and delete the Ⓚ completely.

If you keep going, and cross out your own rack once the bag is empty, you should be left with exactly what's on your opponent's rack.

71 | Check your Averages

You can get a good idea as to how fast your game is improving by working out your average score per (two-player) game – even more useful is finding your average move score.

As a rough guide, you're doing well if you score 300, while 300-350 will see you hold your own at a club, and 350-400 will stand you in good stead at an event. The top players average 400-450.

Scores can vary dramatically depending on the state of the board (open or blocked) and the quality of opponent, which is why average move score is a better indicator. Aim for over 20-points per move – 25 is really good and 30 is excellent.

Doing this can give you a good feel for what to look for from each turn. For instance, if you can only find a score less than 20-points, it might be worth considering changing your letters unless the ones you hold back are so good that you're likely to make up for it with a score of 30-40 on the next turn.

72 UK OK

The odd one out of **ENGLAND**, **IRELAND**, **SCOTLAND** and **WALES** is **IRELAND**, as it's the only one not to have an anagram – surprising with such common letters.

ENGLAND	**ENDLANG**	lengthways
SCOTLAND	**COTLANDS**	cotter's grounds
WALES	**ALEWS**	hunting cries
	SWALE	to sway
	SWEAL	to scorch
	WEALS	raised skin marks

However, **IRELAND** does go with the following letters to make an 8-letter word:

+B	**BILANDER**	small cargo ship
+E	**RENAILED**	
+F	**FILANDER**	kangaroo
+G	**DANGLIER**	
+H	**HARDLINE**	
+N	**INLANDER**	
+S	**ISLANDER**	

Maori Words

There's a plethora of Maori words in the Scrabble 'bible' – here are some really useful fours:

HAKU	the kingfish
HAPU	a subtribe
HIOI	plant of the mint family
HOKA	red cod
KARO	small shrub
KAWA	protocol
KETE	basket
KOHA	gift
KORU	carving pattern
KUIA	elderly woman
KUTU	body louse
MIHA	young fern
MIHI	to greet ceremonially
MIRO	coniferous tree
NAMU	black sandfly
PATU	short club
PUHA	sow thistle
PUKA	tobacco plant
WERO	challenge
WHIO	blue duck

74 **More Maori**

Here's a top twenty of Maori fives – they can often get you out of vowel trouble:

AINGA	village
ARIKI	first-born child
AROHA	love
HIKOI	to protest
HINAU	tree
KANAE	grey mullet
KAURU	edible cabbage stem
KAWAU	black shag
KEHUA	ghost
KIORE	rat
KOURA	crayfish
MAPAU	small tree
MATAI	evergreen tree
MAURI	the soul
MOHUA	small bird
PIKAU	rucksack
POTAE	hat
RAHUI	prohibition
RAUPO	bulrush
TAWAI	beech

T Y P E -cast

There are several kinds of words with the **-TYPE** suffix:

AUTOTYPE	photographic process
BIOTYPE	genetically identical plant group
CEROTYPE	printing plate process
ECOTYPE	group of organisms
GENOTYPE	genetic constitution of organism
HOLOTYPE	original specimen
IDIOTYPE	unique part of antibody
KALOTYPE	early photographic process
LINOTYPE	line of metal type
MONOTYPE	single print
NEOTYPE	replacement specimen
OVERTYPE	to type over existing text
PRETYPE	to type in advance
SEROTYPE	category into which bacterium is placed
TINTYPE	photographic print
VARITYPE	to produce copy
ZOOTYPE	animal figure used as a symbol

76 | Never Say Never

Don't give up if you find yourself a long way behind; part of the beauty of Scrabble is there's nearly always the opportunity to turn it around.

When I was playing in the World Championship Final, I was 177 down and came back to win by 7 points to make the match score 2-2. My opponent was so downhearted that the deciding game was a breeze. Keep positive and believe the 'tile gods' will ultimately favour you – you'll be surprised how often they can.

77 | **Off the Record**

If you are really keen, you could put down all sorts of word lists on tape and play them back to yourself with some uplifting background music. You'll be surprised how many will subconsciously stick.

But beware: this form of practice can be highly dangerous. You would think that long car journeys would be an ideal opportunity to make use of this method, but in my experience you have a high chance of falling asleep at the wheel. Therefore, playback time might be best left for going to bed; it's a great cure for insomnia if nothing else.

78 | **Special Sixes**

If you're ahead in the game, there are some great 6-letter words that are especially useful in acting as blockers as they don't take any hooks at either end. Also, the more letters you play when in front, the sooner you get to the finishing line. Here's an alphabet of examples:

ARGULI	parasites on fish	**MONOAO**	New Zealand plant
BONZER	excellent	**NOGAKU**	Japanese drama
CHANGA	expression of approval	**OCHONE**	expression of regret
DADGUM	damned		
EQUALI	pieces for instruments	**PLONGD**	plunged
		QUOOKE	quaked
FOOBAR	irreparably damaged	**RAWARU**	New Zealand cod
GATVOL	fed up	**SHAZAM**	magic slogan
HUPIRO	offensive-smelling tree	**TIGLIC**	syrupy liquid
		UBIQUE	everywhere
IBIDEM	in the same place	**VERLIG**	enlightened
		WABBIT	weary
JANTEE	sprightly	**XOANON**	carved image of a god
KERERU	New Zealand pigeon		
		YITTEN	frightened
LIKUTA	Zaire coin	**ZAFTIG**	curvaceous

They have the added advantage of potentially lulling your opponent into a mistake by putting an Ⓢ on the end and thereby losing a turn.

Magnificent Sevens

ETAERIO – a kind of fruit – is the most likely 7-letter bonus word to appear on your rack. Here's a taster of some more fruitful 7-letter words made up of the letters you are most likely to draw: A D E I L N O R S T, especially useful when they have no anagram. They are listed in order of probability of being drawn:

ERASION	act of erasing
OTARINE	relating to seals
EROTISE	to make erotic
AIERIES	eagles' nests
TAENIAE	ancient Greek headbands
INOSITE	alcohol
ROSEATE	rose-coloured
SEALINE	sailing company
SENARII	poems
ANISOLE	colourless liquid
ESTRONE	hormone
OLEARIA	daisy bush
RIOTISE	riotous behaviour

ALIENER	one who transfers
EATERIE	restaurant
ARENOSE	sandy
OLEATES	salts of oleic acid
TORNADE	tornado
NEROLIS	oils used in perfumery
AEOLIAN	relating to the wind
OREADES	mountain nymphs
SIENITE	igneous rock
INEDITA	unpublished writings
AEROSAT	communications satellite

Great Eights

AERATION – putting gas into a liquid – is the most commonly played 8-letter word in Scrabble. You'll be surprised how often the following words appear if you hold the right bonus-conducive letters back:

INERTIAE	a plural of inertia
ERIONITE	glassy mineral
AEROLITE	meteorite
AEROTONE	bath with air jets
ERADIATE	radiate
DENTARIA	botanical term
DOUANIER	customs officer
TENORITE	black mineral
TAENIATE	ribbon-like
ETIOLATE	to become weak
LITERATO	literary person
TENTORIA	membranes
RETAILOR	to tailor afresh
ORIENTED	orientated

AURELIAN	person who studies butterflies
DELATION	bringing a charge against
INAURATE	gilded
NOTITIAE	ecclesiastical registers
ETOURDIE	foolish
RITORNEL	orchestral passage
RETINOID	vitamin A derivative
TERATOID	like a monster
INTORTED	twisted inward
TRIENNIA	periods of three years

Even More Hooks

Here are thirty bizarre end hooks to normal 3-letter words that make perfectly valid 4s:

BAG- H	garden	
BED- U	relating to bedouins	
COX- A	hipbone	
DID- O	antic	
FEE- B	contemptible person	
FIX- T	fixed	
GEE- Z	expression of surprise	
GET- A	Japanese sandal	
HER- Y	to praise	
IMP- I	group of Zulu warriors	
JAM- B	to climb a crack in a rock	
KIP- E	basket for catching fish	
LIP- O	liposuction	
MAR- Y	marijuana	

NAB- K	edible berry	
PAW- A	peacock	
PUT- Z	to waste time	
ROT- L	Muslim unit of weight	
SEX- T	noon	
SIT- Z	bath	
TOY- O	Japanese material for making hats	
TRY- E	very good	
UPS- Y	drunken merrymaking	
VAN- G	rope on ship	
VAT- U	monetary unit of Vanuatu	
WAD- T	wad	
WET- A	wingless insect	
YES- K	to hiccup	
YOU- K	to itch	
ZIT- I	pasta	

82 Even More Vowel Trouble

These 4-vowelled 5-letter words are a rarity but extremely useful:

AECIA	structures in fungi
AERIE	eagle's nest
AQUAE	waters
AULOI	ancient Greek pipes
AURAE	a plural of aura
AUREI	Roman coins
LOOIE	lieutenant
LOUIE	"
MIAOU	to meow
OORIE	shabby
OUIJA	spirit board
OURIE	shabby
URAEI	sacred Egyptian serpents
ZOAEA	crab larva
ZOOEA	" "

83 Triple Tactics

The triple-word squares – TWS – are the most bountiful on the board when it comes to points potential. When one becomes available it's often the place to play, but don't get too transfixed by a triple. Some opportunities are better than others depending on your letters. So think very carefully before playing a vowel immediately adjacent to a TWS, but placing a low scoring consonant on the triple line isn't as dangerous as you might think.

Your opponent might score thirty or so points off it, but that's worth the risk if your triple opening move scores far better than any other on the board. You might get unlucky and let them in for a big fifty plus score, or in the worst-case scenario a **triple-triple** or "**9-timer**", where they place their seven letters around the one you've put on the triple line to take in two TWS's for a mammoth move – I once scored 311 with **CONQUEST**. This, however, occurs very rarely and the trick is not to be too paranoid.

So weigh up the odds when opening a TWS – it's worth doing if your score outweighs the give away potential.

If it's your move and a TWS is available, it's the first place you look for, but if you can't make the most of it, don't be afraid to look elsewhere – your opponent may not be able to use it effectively either. An interesting tactic in this instance is to open up a second TWS so you get a share of the spoils on your next turn – risky but fun.

Handy Hindi

There are plenty of Delhi-cious short words originating from India:

DAK	mail	**GORI**	white female (*Hinglish Informal*)
GHI	ghee		
JAI	victory	**KHUD**	ravine
REH	salty crust on soil	**KUTA**	male dog
		KUTI	female dog
SER	unit of weight	**LAKH**	100,000
URD	bean	**LEEP**	to plaster with cow-dung
ANNA	coin		
ARNA	water buffalo	**MALA**	string of beads used in prayer
ARTI	religious ritual		
BABU	Mister	**MOTI**	fat woman
BAEL	spiny tree	**MOWA**	tree
BAPU	spiritual father	**NACH**	dance
BHUT	ghost	**NALA**	ravine
BUDA	old man	**PICE**	coin
BUDI	old woman	**RYOT**	peasant
CHIK	a blind	**SANT**	devout person
DESI	authentic	**TEEK**	well
DHOL	drum	**YAAR**	friend
GORA	white male (*Hinglish Informal*)	**ZILA**	administrative district

More Handy Hindi

Have a Goa at these Indian fives:

AARTI	ceremony with lighted candles
BAJRA	cereal grass
BUNDH	strike
BEEDI	hand rolled cigarette
BIGHA	land measure
CHOLI	blouse
DHUTI	loincloth
DURZI	tailor
GOSHT	meat dish
JAGRA	festival
JOWAR	grass
KHADI	cotton cloth
LUNGI	long cloth
MANDI	big market
PIPUL	fig tree
RATHA	carriage
SWAMI	mystic
TAVAH	frying pan
THAGI	thuggery
TONGA	two-wheeled vehicle
YOJAN	unit of distance

Rising to the Challenge

In UK Scrabble you've got nothing to lose by challenging a word you don't know, whereas in the US if the word turns out to be OK, you lose your next turn. There's something aesthetically unpleasing about non-words staying on the board, but it's surprising how often it happens. **Don't be afraid to challenge**: if you have a scintilla of doubt, look it up. There's nothing more frustrating than letting a word go and finding it's not in the dictionary when it's too late. It might seem obvious when the challenges are 'free', but it's surprising how often players feel too embarrassed or intimidated to check.

As a general rule, challenge anything you wouldn't be sure of playing yourself.

87 Vanquish the V

Vs are horrible and should be discarded at the earliest opportunity. Here are forty voluptuous 3- and 4-letter V-words to assist you:

DEV	divine being
EVO	evening
LUV	love
SAV	saveloy
UVA	grape
VAC	to vacuum
VAV	Hebrew letter
VAW	Hebrew letter
VIG	interest on loan
VOE	small bay
VOL	volume
VOR	to warn
VUG	small rock cavity
VUM	to swear
GYVE	to shackle
KAVA	Polynesian shrub
OMOV	one member one vote
RIVO	informal toast
TAVA	Indian frying pan

ULVA	seaweed
VAGI	cranial nerves
VANG	rope on ship
VAUT	vault
VEEP	vice president
VEHM	medieval German court
VERD	marble
VEXT	vexed
VIBS	climbing shoes
VILD	vile
VITE	musical direction
VIVA	to examine in a spoken interview
VIVE	long live
VIVO	with vigour
VIZY	to look
VLEI	low marshy ground
VOLK	nation
VRIL	life force
VROU	woman
VUGH	small rock cavity
VULN	to wound

U don't want to be with a W

Two letters that are awful together are the U and W – there are a few words to help get rid of them both in one turn:

WUD	wood	**UNWIT**	to divest of wit
WUS	term of address	**UNWON**	not won
WAUK	full cloth	**VROUW**	woman
WAUL	to cry like a cat	**WAUFF**	to flutter
WAUR	war	**WAUGH**	to bark
WHUP	to defeat totally	**WAULK**	full cloth
		WHUMP	to make a dull thud
WUDU	ritual washing	**WOFUL**	woeful
WULL	will	**WURST**	large sausage
DWAUM	to faint	**WUSHU**	Chinese martial arts
SWOUN	swoon		
UNWED	not wed	**WUSSY**	feeble
UNWET	not wet	**WUXIA**	Chinese film

89 | **Off the Hook**

There are some surprising hooks you can play on the end of regular 2-letter words as well:

GO-	A	Tibetan gazelle	WE-	M	womb
MI-	B	a marble	GO-	N	geometrical grade
TO-	C	signal for letter t	EX-	O	excellent
LO-	D	logarithm	HE-	P	hip
HI-	E	to hurry	LA-	R	young man
DO-	F	stupid	BY-	S	bye
ME-	G	megabyte	AT-	T	Siamese coin
NO-	H	Japanese drama	AM-	U	unit of mass
MO-	I	me	PA-	V	pavlova
HA-	J	Muslim pilgrimage	MA-	W	to bite
TA-	K	take	SO-	X	socks
DO-	L	unit of pain intensity	HO-	Y	drive animal with cry
			RE-	Z	reservation

The only 3-letter word ending in Q is **SUQ** – a Muslim market place – sadly this isn't a hook as **SU** isn't a word, but it's still extremely useful.

90 Angry Words

ANGRIEST is the most productive 8-letter anagram combination:

ANGSTIER   more anxious
ASTRINGE   to cause contraction
GANISTER   sedimentary rock
GANTRIES
GRANITES
INGRATES   ungrateful people
RANGIEST
REASTING   being noisily uncooperative
STEARING   steering
TASERING   using a Taser gun

It's not that important to know all the anagrams – the more the better – but if you know two or three, you're more than likely to be able to fit one of them on the board.

W I S E Words

A few **-WISE** words to end our suffix sojourn:

ARCHWISE	like an arch
BENDWISE	diagonally
CRABWISE	sideways
DROPWISE	in form of a drop
EDGEWISE	edgeways
FANWISE	like a fan
LONGWISE	lengthways
MANWISE	in human way
OVERWISE	too wise
PALEWISE	by perpendicular lines
RINGWISE	experienced in the ring
SOMEWISE	to some degree
TENTWISE	in the manner of a tent
WARPWISE	in the direction of the warp

Interestingly, **WISEMAN** is not allowed but **WISEWOMAN** is – it means a witch.

92 Fatherly Advice

PATERNAL has two appropriate anagrams –
PARENTAL and **PRENATAL** – speaking of which there's
also **PARLANTE**.

The only one that takes an [S] is **PRENATAL**, as in a prenatal
examination.

93 | ZZZS

Respect your opponent by not playing too slowly. A good average time to play each move is about two minutes – in tournament play, chess clocks are used and you're allowed twenty-five minutes to play all your moves – since each game lasts an average of about thirteen moves each, you're looking at just under two minutes for each turn.

Some moves are more difficult than others, so it's fair enough to take longer sometimes, but anything in excess of five minutes and you're likely to send your opponent to sleep. The only time I have ever played my wife I dropped off due to her slow play and we never finished the game.

If you use a clock, the rule is that you lose 10 points for every minute (or part thereof) that you go over the twenty-five minute deadline. There was a rather elderly chap in the States who was 250-points ahead in his game, when he started snoring – his devious opponent realised his only chance of winning was to let him stay asleep and the poor man apparently went over on his clock by twenty-five minutes. He woke up to find that his 250-point lead had been cancelled out, but just in time to play the winning move: justice done.

By the way **ZZZS** is actually a valid word – the last in the dictionary – though you'd have to use both blanks to play it as there's only one Z in the set.

94 Hook, Line and Sinker

The final word on the hooks is left to these fabulous front hooks of 7-letter words to make fantastic 8s:

A -DUSTING	drying up by heat
B -ARTISAN	small turret
C -UNIFORM	ancient writing system
D -HURRIES	Indian cotton carpet
E -RODENTS	things that wear away
F -UGLIEST	extremely ugly
G -ELASTIC	relating to laughter
H -EXAMINE	type of fuel
I -CONICAL	relating to an icon
J -AUNTIES	naval masters-at-arms
K -VETCHES	grumbles
L -IGNEOUS	like wood
M -UNITING	strengthening
N -OVATION	substitution of a new obligation
O -DONATES	dragonflies
P -LUMBAGO	plant
R -ENFORCE	reinforce
S -CHILLER	unusual mineral lustre
T -HERMITS	processes for reducing metallic oxides
U -PLAYING	stashing
V -ROOMING	moving noisily at high speed
W -INDIGOS	cannibals
Y -EARLIES	once a year events
Z -INKIEST	most like zinc

Superstitions

You don't need to wear 666 across your forehead or bring in a black cat, but if you think a certain superstition brings you luck, use it – for the power of positive thinking if nothing else.

When I won the World Championship, I found I was on a winning run after using the same toilet cubicle in between games – I would go through the same routine every time, but it became rather embarrassing when someone was already in there and I hung around the bathroom waiting for them to finish – I remember getting several strange looks from other users of the facilities.

Even so, anything that gives you a good vibe is worth pursuing.

Do You Feel Lucky?

Part of the beauty of Scrabble is that, with some good fortune, nearly anyone can beat anyone. However, luck does not play as big a part in the game as you might think. It is no coincidence that the weakest players are the ones who tend to blame their luck the most.

Nigel Richards, the World Champion in 2007 and regarded by many as the best player in the world, never curses his luck. He has won countless tournaments and almost invariably features in the top five of any event. Skill in Scrabble far outweighs fortune – the more you moan about your letters, the worse they are likely to get – negativity breeds negativity so avoid it all costs.

You can certainly **make your own luck** in the game by giving yourself opportunities that others might not spot – it doesn't pay off all the time, but it will count in the long run.

The biggest luck element comes in picking up most of the blanks and **S**s – the best tiles in the set. Even then, you can increase your chances of getting these by simply playing more letters than your opponent, which is a skill in itself.

Over a lot of games, the better players always rise to the top, but if you're evenly matched, a little bit of luck can make all the difference.

New Additions

Every five years or so, the dictionary is updated and the latest edition contains over 1500 new words up to eight letters in length. These will be recognised in official tournament play from January 2012, but there's no reason why you can't play them sooner if you can't wait.

Forty fabulous new favourites follow:

ALU	potato in Indian cookery
AWFY	awfully
BOOAI	thoroughly lost
CAPEX	capital expenditure
CEZVE	small metal coffee pot
DARTITIS	nervous twitch while playing darts
DOOBRIE	thingumabob
ERM	expression of hesitation
FILII	sons
FIQH	Islamic jurisprudence
GHUBAR	numeral
GNATWREN	small bird
GRRL	young woman who enjoys aggressively feminist punk rock
HETTIE	heterosexual
ING	meadow near a river
JULIET	code word for letter J
KILOPOND	unit of gravitational force

LIFEHACK	action reducing frustration in everyday life
MANKINI	a revealing man's swimming costume
MOOBS	overdeveloped breasts on a man
MWAH	sound of a fake kiss
NGAI	tribe
NOOB	person new to a job
OFFIE	off-licence
PERMATAN	permanent artificial tan
PHWOAR	expression of sexual attraction
QIN	Chinese stringed instrument
RAV	rabbi
SHEMALE	male who has acquired female characteristics through surgery
SOZ	sorry
SPORK	cross between spoon and fork
TEALIGHT	small candle
UMMA	Muslim community
VISHING	telephone scam
VLOG	video weblog
WAGYU	Japanese breed of beef cattle
WEBISODE	TV episode for online viewing
XRAY	code word for letter X
YUPSTER	person who combines a lucrative career with non-mainstream tastes
ZARI	thread made from gold or silver wire

98 | Eliminate the Page

If you are enthusiastic enough to look at some word lists, a good way to study is to remove the words you are sure you have mastered by deleting them with a black marker pen.

Each time you go back to the relevant page, you'll be able to remove more by recognition, so it will continually seem less daunting to study until you ultimately eliminate the whole page – this is a very satisfying and positive way to learn and move on.

99 Consonant Dumps

If you hold six or seven consonants on you rack, you'll be looking to restore the balance.

These 2- and 3-letter consonant-only words will help:

CH	eke
FY	fie
KY	cows
NY	nigh
HM	hesitation
MM	enjoyment
BRR	shivering
CLY	to steal
CWM	steep-sided hollow
GYP	to cheat
HMM	more hesitation
HYP	hypotenuse
LYM	leash
MYC	gene causing tumours
PHT	irritation
RHY	rye
SWY	Australian gambling game
SYN	since
TWP	stupid
TYG	mug with two handles
VLY	low marshy ground
WYN	Germanic character equivalent to W

98 Eliminate the Page

If you are enthusiastic enough to look at some word lists, a good way to study is to remove the words you are sure you have mastered by deleting them with a black marker pen.

Each time you go back to the relevant page, you'll be able to remove more by recognition, so it will continually seem less daunting to study until you ultimately eliminate the whole page – this is a very satisfying and positive way to learn and move on.

99 Consonant Dumps

If you hold six or seven consonants on you rack, you'll be looking to restore the balance.

These 2- and 3-letter consonant-only words will help:

CH	eke
FY	fie
KY	cows
NY	nigh
HM	hesitation
MM	enjoyment
BRR	shivering
CLY	to steal
CWM	steep-sided hollow
GYP	to cheat
HMM	more hesitation
HYP	hypotenuse
LYM	leash
MYC	gene causing tumours
PHT	irritation
RHY	rye
SWY	Australian gambling game
SYN	since
TWP	stupid
TYG	mug with two handles
VLY	low marshy ground
WYN	Germanic character equivalent to W

4- and 5-letter words to alleviate a consonant crisis:

BRRR	more shivering	**SKYF**	to smoke a cigarette
BYRL	to remove lumps in cloth	**SKYR**	Scandinavian cheese
FYRD	Anglo-Saxon militia	**SYPH**	syphilis
GYMP	to limp	**TRYP**	parasite
GYNY	gynaecology	**TYMP**	blast furnace outlet
HWYL	emotional fervour		
KYND	kind	**TYPP**	unit of thickness of yarn
LYCH	dead body		
PFFT	sudden disappearance	**TYPY**	typifying breed of animal
RYND	crossbar part of millstone		
SCRY	to divine by crystal gazing	**WYCH**	tree
		WYND	narrow lane
SKRY	to try to tell future	**XYST**	long portico
		YMPT	repaired birds' wings

Watch out for **CRWTH**, an ancient stringed Celtic instrument, and **CWTCH** – to be snuggled up – there's also the unlikely **PHPHT**, which expresses irritation.

101 | **The Endgame**

Making the most of the **endgame** is worthy of a book in itself. A few principles to follow once the bag is empty are:

(a) Assuming you can't use all your letters in one go, try to find a way of playing out in two turns, to give yourself the best chance of playing the last move of the game.

(b) Score as many points as possible over the two turns, ideally at the same time stopping your opponent from getting their best score or from playing out (you'll know their letters and what they can potentially play if you've tile tracked correctly).

(c) Think hard about which order to play the two turns in – it's often best to save the best to last and take the lower scoring move first, particularly if it stymies your opponent.

(d) If possible, set up a big scoring final move with your penultimate turn – especially if your opponent can't block it – even if they can, they may have to sacrifice vital points to do so.

(e) Bear in mind your **penultimate move** is really the most important of the whole game since it's the only one in which you can decide your next turn as well.

(f) In close games, the **endgame** is all-important – it's amazing how many wins you can eke out from a seemingly forlorn position – never give up.

Four Nights in Bangkok

If you're getting eager and fancy trying out an international (English speaking) Scrabble tournament, I would highly recommend the "King's Cup" in Bangkok – effectively Thailand's national championship. Held every June, this is an incredible event, open to everyone. It takes place in the National Stadium, which is the only place big enough to accommodate the ever-increasing number of participants (it's getting close to 10,000).

There is an opening ceremony which features dancing girls and players welcomed on stage with their national flags. Then there's some pretty intense Scrabble for four days while the atmosphere positively buzzes, culminating in the finalists being serenaded to the sound of Queen's "We are the Champions".

The winner gets a cheque for $10,000 from a member of Thailand's royal family and, if they are sensible, goes for a well-earned rest on one of Thailand's fantastic islands for a couple of weeks.

There's a host of other events on the international calendar – to find out more, take a look at the World English-language Scrabble Players' Association (WESPA) website – **www.wespa.org**

103 OVER.....

You can get too much of a good thing with some of these:

OVERABLE	**OVERMILK**
OVERBIG	**OVERNET**
OVERCOY	**OVERPLUS**
OVERDUST	**OVERRUDE**
OVEREGG	**OVERSUDS**
OVERFISH	**OVERTART**
OVERGILD	**OVERURGE**
OVERHOLY	**OVERVEIL**
OVERIDLE	**OVERWILY**
OVERJUST	**OVERYEAR**
OVERKNEE	**OVERZEAL**
OVERLEWD	

Here are some more out-standing words:

OUTADDS

OUTBITCH

OUTCHEAT

OUTDREAM

OUTECHO

OUTFLASH

OUTGNAW

OUTHOWL

OUTJINX

OUTKISS

OUTLOVE

OUTMARCH

OUTNAME

OUTPITY

OUTQUOTE

OUTRING

OUTSIZE

OUTTHROB

OUTVENOM

OUTWHIRL

OUTYELL

And so to ZED

There are some lovely 3-letter words involving the Z:

ADZ	adze	**WIZ**	wizard
BEZ	part of deer's horn	**ZAG**	to change direction sharply
BIZ	business	**ZAX**	saxophone
CAZ	casual	**ZEA**	corn silk
COZ	cousin	**ZEE**	the letter Z
CUZ	cousin	**ZEK**	Soviet prisoner
FIZ	fizz		
JIZ	wig	**ZEP**	long sandwich
LEZ	lesbian (*slang*)	**ZEX**	cutting tool
LUZ	indestructible human bone	**ZIG**	to change direction sharply
MIZ	misery		
MOZ	jinx	**ZIN**	zinfandel
POZ	positive	**ZIT**	pimple
RIZ	past form of rise	**ZOA**	independent animal bodies
SAZ	Middle Eastern instrument	**ZOL**	cannabis cigarette
SEZ	says		

Keep looking to play the Z across and down simultaneously on the premium squares – double gets you forty points, triple scores a hefty sixty.

Worth a Read and a Watch

"Word Freak – Heartbreak, Triumph, Genius and Obsession in the World of Competitive Scrabble Players" is a best-selling book by Wall Street journalist Stefan Fatsis. It tells of an ordinary guy starting out in the 'Scrabble World' and is a really excellent read – the film rights have been bought by Curtis Hanson – director of "LA Confidential".

"Word Wars – Tiles and Tribulations on the Scrabble Game Circuit" is a great real-life documentary by Eric Chaikin, focusing on four top US Scrabblers – it's very funny and well worth watching.

If more comprehensive word-lists take your fancy, "Official Scrabble Lists" by Collins is the book to buy, while "Scrabble Words" is the official word list minus the meanings.

If you insist on the definitions, there's always Collins Dictionary to while away the time.

If you fancy a bit of variety, Bananagrams, Boggle, Channel 4's Countdown and Scrabble Trickster are all good Scrabble practice. A very useful online medium is Jumble Time, in which you have to break down a 'wall' of anagrams within a certain time – either individually or against multi-opponents – this can be found at **www.jumbletime.com** and is really great fun.

Facebook Scrabble is all the rage these days – you can have as many simultaneous games as you like against players of a similar standard – very sociable and highly addictive.

Taking it Further

There are over 300 Scrabble clubs in the UK, normally meeting weekly with an average membership of fifteen. Two or three games are played over an evening in a variety of venues ranging from homes to pubs to village halls, and there are competitions, leagues and trophies to be won over a season.

Joining a club is the first step towards Scrabble seriousness and can be quite daunting to start with – just remember the vast majority of club players are extremely pleasant and don't be put off by the over competitive minority.

There is a Scrabble event to be found somewhere in the UK on almost every weekend of the year.

The numbers of players can range from ten to a hundred, and the larger tournaments contain more than one division, so you're placed with players of a similar standard. There are usually six or seven games in a one-day event – weekends can take in around sixteen.

If you don't take it too seriously they can be great fun – the only big difference from playing at home or at a club is the use of timers to ensure the games last under an hour and no one holds up the schedule – they don't take long to get used to operating.

The ABSP is the Association of British Scrabble Players and is effectively the game's governing body.

It costs £15/year to join (there are about 800 members), and for that you get an excellent bi-monthly newsletter and various tournament discounts. The ABSP website can be found at **www.absp.org.uk** and contains everything you need to know about what's going on in the 'Scrabble World'. There's a tournament calendar, event results, rankings and word-lists and plenty of other useful material for the aspiring player.

If you are interested in joining a Scrabble club you can get in touch with Scrabble Clubs UK – scrabbleuk@mattel. com.

The 124 two-letter words playable in Scrabble are...

AA	CH	GO	LO	OO	TO
AB	DA	GU	MA	OP	UG
AD	DE	HA	ME	OR	UH
AE	DI	HE	MI	OS	UM
AG	DO	HI	MM	OU	UN
AH	EA	HM	MO	OW	UP
AI	ED	HO	MU	OX	UR
AL	EE	ID	MY	OY	US
AM	EF	IF	NA	PA	UT
AN	EH	IN	NE	PE	WE
AR	EL	IO	NO	PI	WO
AS	EM	IS	NU	PO	XI
AT	EN	IT	NY	QI	XU
AW	ER	JA	OB	RE	YA
AX	ES	JO	OD	SH	YE
AY	ET	KA	OE	SI	YO
BA	EX	KI	OF	SO	YU
BE	FA	KO	OH	ST	ZA
BI	FE	KY	OI	TA	ZO
BO	FY	LA	OM	TE	
BY	GI	LI	ON	TI	

The 1310 three-letter words playable in Scrabble are...

AAH	AIA	ANA	ASP	BAD	BIO
AAL	AID	AND	ASS	BAG	BIS
AAS	AIL	ANE	ATE	BAH	BIT
ABA	AIM	ANI	ATS	BAL	BIZ
ABB	AIN	ANN	ATT	BAM	BOA
ABO	AIR	ANS	AUA	BAN	BOB
ABS	AIS	ANT	AUE	BAP	BOD
ABY	AIT	ANY	AUF	BAR	BOG
ACE	AKA	APE	AUK	BAS	BOH
ACH	AKE	APO	AVA	BAT	BOI
ACT	ALA	APP	AVE	BAY	BOK
ADD	ALB	APT	AVO	BED	BON
ADO	ALE	ARB	AWA	BEE	BOO
ADS	ALF	ARC	AWE	BEG	BOP
ADZ	ALL	ARD	AWK	BEL	BOR
AFF	ALP	ARE	AWL	BEN	BOS
AFT	ALS	ARF	AWN	BES	BOT
AGA	ALT	ARK	AXE	BET	BOW
AGE	ALU	ARM	AYE	BEY	BOX
AGO	AMA	ARS	AYS	BEZ	BOY
AGS	AME	ART	AYU	BIB	BRA
AHA	AMI	ARY	AZO	BID	BRO
AHI	AMP	ASH	BAA	BIG	BRR
AHS	AMU	ASK	BAC	BIN	BRU

BUB	CHI	CUT	DID	DSO	EFS
BUD	CID	CUZ	DIE	DUB	EFT
BUG	CIG	CWM	DIF	DUD	EGG
BUM	CIS	DAB	DIG	DUE	EGO
BUN	CIT	DAD	DIM	DUG	EHS
BUR	CLY	DAE	DIN	DUH	EIK
BUS	COB	DAG	DIP	DUI	EKE
BUT	COD	DAH	DIS	DUN	ELD
BUY	COG	DAK	DIT	DUO	ELF
BYE	COL	DAL	DIV	DUP	ELK
BYS	CON	DAM	DOB	DUX	ELL
CAA	COO	DAN	DOC	DYE	ELM
CAB	COP	DAP	DOD	DZO	ELS
CAD	COR	DAS	DOE	EAN	ELT
CAG	COS	DAW	DOF	EAR	EME
CAM	COT	DAY	DOG	EAS	EMO
CAN	COW	DEB	DOH	EAT	EMS
CAP	COX	DEE	DOL	EAU	EMU
CAR	COY	DEF	DOM	EBB	END
CAT	COZ	DEG	DON	ECH	ENE
CAW	CRU	DEI	DOO	ECO	ENG
CAY	CRY	DEL	DOP	ECU	ENS
CAZ	CUB	DEN	DOR	EDH	EON
CEE	CUD	DEV	DOS	EDS	ERA
CEL	CUE	DEW	DOT	EEK	ERE
CEP	CUM	DEX	DOW	EEL	ERF
CHA	CUP	DEY	DOY	EEN	ERG
CHE	CUR	DIB	DRY	EFF	ERK

ERM	FAX	FOE	GAS	GOB	HAJ
ERN	FAY	FOG	GAT	GOD	HAM
ERR	FED	FOH	GAU	GOE	HAN
ERS	FEE	FON	GAW	GON	HAO
ESS	FEG	FOP	GAY	GOO	HAP
EST	FEH	FOR	GED	GOR	HAS
ETA	FEM	FOU	GEE	GOS	HAT
ETH	FEN	FOX	GEL	GOT	HAW
EUK	FER	FOY	GEM	GOV	HAY
EVE	FES	FRA	GEN	GOX	HEH
EVO	FET	FRO	GEO	GOY	HEM
EWE	FEU	FRY	GER	GUB	HEN
EWK	FEW	FUB	GET	GUE	HEP
EWT	FEY	FUD	GEY	GUL	HER
EXO	FEZ	FUG	GHI	GUM	HES
EYE	FIB	FUM	GIB	GUN	HET
FAA	FID	FUN	GID	GUP	HEW
FAB	FIE	FUR	GIE	GUR	HEX
FAD	FIG	GAB	GIF	GUS	HEY
FAE	FIL	GAD	GIG	GUT	HIC
FAG	FIN	GAE	GIN	GUV	HID
FAH	FIR	GAG	GIO	GUY	HIE
FAN	FIT	GAK	GIP	GYM	HIM
FAP	FIX	GAL	GIS	GYP	HIN
FAR	FIZ	GAM	GIT	HAD	HIP
FAS	FLU	GAN	GJU	HAE	HIS
FAT	FLY	GAP	GNU	HAG	HI
FAW	FOB	GAR	GOA	HAH	HMM

HOA	ICE	JAG	JUT	KIT	LEE
HOB	ICH	JAI	KAB	KOA	LEG
HOC	ICK	JAK	KAE	KOB	LEI
HOD	ICY	JAM	KAF	KOI	LEK
HOE	IDE	JAP	KAI	KON	LEP
HOG	IDS	JAR	KAK	KOP	LES
HOH	IFF	JAW	KAM	KOR	LET
HOI	IFS	JAY	KAS	KOS	LEU
HOM	IGG	JEE	KAT	KOW	LEV
HON	ILK	JET	KAW	KUE	LEW
HOO	ILL	JEU	KAY	KYE	LEX
HOP	IMP	JEW	KEA	KYU	LEY
HOS	ING	JIB	KEB	LAB	LEZ
HOT	INK	JIG	KED	LAC	LIB
HOW	INN	JIN	KEF	LAD	LID
HOX	INS	JIZ	KEG	LAG	LIE
HOY	ION	JOB	KEN	LAH	LIG
HUB	IOS	JOE	KEP	LAM	LIN
HUE	IRE	JOG	KET	LAP	LIP
HUG	IRK	JOL	KEX	LAR	LIS
HUH	ISH	JOR	KEY	LAS	LIT
HUI	ISM	JOT	KHI	LAT	LOB
HUM	ISO	JOW	KID	LAV	LOD
HUN	ITA	JOY	KIF	LAW	LOG
HUP	ITS	JUD	KIN	LAX	LOO
HUT	IVY	JUG	KIP	LAY	LOP
HYE	IWI	JUN	KIR	LEA	LOR
HYP	JAB	JUS	KIS	LED	LOS

LOT	MAX	MOD	NAM	NOH	OCH
LOU	MAY	MOE	NAN	NOM	ODA
LOW	MED	MOG	NAP	NON	ODD
LOX	MEE	MOI	NAS	NOO	ODE
LOY	MEG	MOL	NAT	NOR	ODS
LUD	MEH	MOM	NAW	NOS	OES
LUG	MEL	MON	NAY	NOT	OFF
LUM	MEM	MOO	NEB	NOW	OFT
LUR	MEN	MOP	NED	NOX	OHM
LUV	MES	MOR	NEE	NOY	OHO
LUX	MET	MOS	NEF	NTH	OHS
LUZ	MEU	MOT	NEG	NUB	OIK
LYE	MEW	MOU	NEK	NUN	OIL
LYM	MHO	MOW	NEP	NUR	OIS
MAA	MIB	MOY	NET	NUS	OKA
MAC	MIC	MOZ	NEW	NUT	OKE
MAD	MID	MUD	NIB	NYE	OLD
MAE	MIG	MUG	NID	NYS	OLE
MAG	MIL	MUM	NIE	OAF	OLM
MAK	MIM	MUN	NIL	OAK	OMS
MAL	MIR	MUS	NIM	OAR	ONE
MAM	MIS	MUT	NIP	OAT	ONO
MAN	MIX	MUX	NIS	OBA	ONS
MAP	MIZ	MYC	NIT	OBE	ONY
MAR	MNA	NAB	NIX	OBI	OOF
MAS	MOA	NAE	NOB	OBO	OOH
MAT	MOB	NAG	NOD	OBS	OOM
MAW	MOC	NAH	NOG	OCA	OON

OOP	OXY	PET	POW	RAH	REX
OOR	OYE	PEW	POX	RAI	REZ
OOS	OYS	PHI	POZ	RAJ	RHO
OOT	PAC	PHO	PRE	RAM	RHY
OPE	PAD	PHT	PRO	RAN	RIA
OPS	PAH	PIA	PRY	RAP	RIB
OPT	PAL	PIC	PSI	RAS	RID
ORA	PAM	PIE	PST	RAT	RIF
ORB	PAN	PIG	PUB	RAV	RIG
ORC	PAP	PIN	PUD	RAW	RIM
ORD	PAR	PIP	PUG	RAX	RIN
ORE	PAS	PIR	PUH	RAY	RIP
ORF	PAT	PIS	PUL	REB	RIT
ORS	PAV	PIT	PUN	REC	RIZ
ORT	PAW	PIU	PUP	RED	ROB
OSE	PAX	PIX	PUR	REE	ROC
OUD	PAY	PLU	PUS	REF	ROD
OUK	PEA	PLY	PUT	REG	ROE
OUP	PEC	POA	PUY	REH	ROK
OUR	PED	POD	PYA	REI	ROM
OUS	PEE	POH	PYE	REM	ROO
OUT	PEG	POI	PYX	REN	ROT
OVA	PEH	POL	QAT	REO	ROW
OWE	PEL	POM	QIN	REP	RUB
OWL	PEN	POO	QIS	RES	RUC
OWN	PEP	POP	QUA	RET	RUD
OWT	PER	POS	RAD	REV	RUE
OXO	PES	POT	RAG	REW	RUG